Mastering Critical Thinking:

The Art of Logical Problem Solving

By

Brad M. Godfrey

TABLE OF CONTENTS

INTRODUCTION

The capacity to think critically is more vital now than it has ever been in a society that is constantly overloaded with information, is always changing, and makes difficult decisions. The ability to think logically, creatively, and strategically can be the deciding factor in whether or not you are successful in a variety of challenging situations, including those in which you are trying to solve a challenging problem at work, trying to make a difficult personal decision or simply attempting to navigate the often-murky waters of modern media and information.

The mastery of critical thinking is thus necessary for this context. It's the skill of employing reasoning, analysis, and assessment to zero in on the most important concerns, sort through the available data, and arrive at judgments that are rational and well-informed. It is a talent that can be taught, refined, and used in a wide variety of situations, including the workplace, personal relationships, societal concerns, and political disputes. It is a skill that can be learned, honed, and applied.

In this book, we will discuss the fundamentals of critical thinking and give you techniques, tools, and methods that may be put into practice to build and improve your critical thinking abilities. You will gain the ability to recognize important issues, collect and assess information, conduct analyses of data, and come to sensible conclusions based on rigorous thinking and logical approaches to addressing problems.

This book will provide you with the tools and insights you need to succeed in a world that demands thoughtful, strategic, and effective decision-making. Whether you are a student, a professional, or simply someone looking to improve your critical thinking abilities, this book will provide you with the tools and insights you need to succeed. Now that we have everything out of the way let's get started learning how to think critically!

CHAPTER ONE

What is Critical Thinking?

Critical thinking is a mental process that involves examining, evaluating, and synthesizing information in order to make conclusions and choices that are supported by logic and reasoning. It is a talent that is vital in the world that we live in today, which is complicated and continuously changing, where we are constantly being barraged with information and where we are forced to make challenging choices.

Before coming to a decision, critical thinking requires one to first engage in a series of activities, including formulating questions, collecting and analyzing information, and considering a variety of points of view. It demands a willingness to question presumptions, investigate other explanations, and assess the benefits and drawbacks of various solutions.

Being critical or skeptical is just one aspect of critical thinking; the two go hand in hand. It's about having an open mind, being interested, and being ready to shift your perspective depending on new information. It requires the ability to understand your own prejudices and limits, in addition to those of others, as well as those of yourself.

The ability to think is useful in a wide variety of circumstances, ranging from academic and professional environments to one's own personal decision-making. It may help us negotiate difficult problems such as politics, ethics, and social justice, and it can also assist us in making better decisions about our health, our money, and the relationships we have.

In general, critical thinking is a talent that can be acquired through practice and experience, and it is a skill that may be very important. It demands a devotion to intellectual curiosity, a readiness to ask challenging questions, and a determination to search for and assess the evidence. We have the ability to become more educated, involved, and productive members of our communities as well as society as a whole if we develop our critical thinking abilities.

The Importance of Critical Thinking
The Value of Critical Reasoning

. The ability to think critically is a crucial talent that enables humans to examine, assess, and interpret information in a way that is logical and consistent. A cognitive process that lets humans solve issues make educated judgments, and construct informed views based on facts and reasoning. It is a cognitive process that enables individuals to make sensible decisions. Critical thinking is becoming more crucial for people to possess in the complicated and fast-paced world of today so that they can navigate through the vast amounts of information and make sense of it.

Critical thinking helps people to assess the benefits and drawbacks of a variety of possibilities in order to arrive at well-informed conclusions, which is a necessary component of effective decision-making. When making a choice, it is beneficial for people to assess information in an impartial manner and to take into account all pertinent considerations.

Individuals are better able to recognize and comprehend challenges, as well as come up with workable answers when they have developed their critical thinking skills. It liberates people to think creatively and unconventionally, allowing them to come up with novel approaches to problems.

Increased effectiveness in communication: Those that engage in critical thinking are able to improve their ability to communicate by expressing their thoughts in a way that is crystal clear, logical, and consistent. It is beneficial to people because it enables them to analyze the validity of arguments and appraise the strengths and weaknesses of other points of view.

Improved judgment comes from engaging in critical thinking, which enables people to differentiate between reality and fiction, as well as detect information that is erroneous or misleading. It enables people to challenge their preconceived notions and preconceived prejudices and to generate educated opinions on the basis of facts and reasoning.

Learning throughout one's life: persons who practice critical thinking are more likely to be motivated to seek out new knowledge and points of view and to participate in continuous learning. It assists people in evaluating the quality and dependability of sources of information and in making educated choices about what to learn and how to study it in a manner that is most effective for them.

Capacity for Adaptation: Critical thinking equips people with the capacity to adjust to shifting conditions and think creatively on their feet. It gives people the ability to assess new information and alter both their ideas and behaviors in response to that knowledge.

Those that are able to innovate via the use of critical thinking are able to produce fresh ideas and views. It encourages people to think creatively and assists them in developing novel approaches to solving difficult situations.

Critical thinking is regarded as a vital talent for success in many different industries, and companies place a high value on employees who demonstrate this ability. Those who are able to demonstrate good critical thinking abilities have a greater chance of being employed, advanced in their jobs, and achieving professional success.

Personal development: the ability to think critically may pave the way for one's own development and advancement. It gives people the opportunity to evaluate their own views and assumptions and to come up with fresh understandings and points of view.

Thinking critically is a need for democratic citizenship, hence democratic citizenship requires critical thinking. It enables people to establish objective assessments of political and social problems, engage actively in civic life, and take choices based on accurate information.

Critical thinking helps people to make ethical judgments by analyzing the influence of their actions on others and contemplating the ethical implications of their choices. This evaluation is a necessary step in the process of ethical decision-making.

In the field of science, the ability to think critically is very necessary. It enables humans to assess facts in a neutral manner, make inferences based on logic, and arrive at reasonable judgments.

Critical Thinking and Problem-Solving

Critical thinking and the ability to solve problems are two talents that are inextricably linked and are absolutely necessary for success in the complicated and fast-paced world of today. Those that possess these talents are able to assess, comprehend, and analyze information, as well as come up with efficient solutions to issues.

The cognitive process known as critical thinking is doing an objective analysis of information, taking into account all relevant elements, and arriving at well-informed conclusions on the basis of facts and logic. It gives people the ability to challenge assumptions, analyze arguments, and recognize biases and logical errors in their own thinking. Those who engage in critical thinking are better able to think creatively and devise original solutions to difficult situations than those who do not.

On the other hand, problem-solving entails locating and examining issues, as well as conceptualizing and implementing workable solutions. Before coming up with a solution, people need to engage in analytical thinking, conduct an impartial analysis of the circumstance, and take into account all of the essential aspects. Individuals must also be creative and imaginative in the manner in which they approach problem-solving, and they must be prepared to experiment with different approaches in the event that the first strategy is unsuccessful.

The link between critical thinking and the ability to solve problems is one that is mutually supportive and beneficial. Those that are capable of critical thinking are able to successfully recognize and analyze issues, as well as assess alternative solutions in an impartial manner. Problem-solving, on the other hand, requires the use of critical thinking abilities in order to analyze the circumstance, devise a course of action, and assess the efficiency of the solution.

The following is a list of examples of how analytical thinking and the ability to solve problems may be utilized in a variety of contexts:

The ability to think critically and effectively solve problems is very necessary for success in the corporate world. Those who possess these talents are able to recognize and assess issues that arise in business, evaluate the viability of prospective solutions, and devise strategies that are beneficial in achieving company objectives. In addition, analytical thinking and the ability to solve problems are essential for innovation and being ahead of one's competition in a corporate climate that is always changing.

In the field of education, the ability to think critically and solve problems is very necessary for success. Students that have these abilities are able to effectively examine information, assess arguments and evidence, and generate effective solutions to issues that arise in the classroom. The ability to think critically and solve problems is also essential for continuing education and for one's own personal development.

Critical thinking and the ability to solve problems are crucial skills for anyone working in the healthcare industry. These abilities enable healthcare practitioners to successfully assess patient data, evaluate treatment alternatives, and design treatment strategies for patients. Critical thinking and the ability to solve problems are also essential components of successful research and innovation in the healthcare industry.

The ability to think critically and effectively solve problems is very necessary for a career in government. These abilities provide government officials the ability to examine policy problems, evaluate alternative solutions, and design policies that are both successful and beneficial to society. The ability to think critically and effectively solve problems is another skill that is essential for democratic citizenship and active engagement in governance.

In the field of science, being able to think critically and solve problems is very necessary for success. These abilities enable scientists to successfully examine data, assess evidence and arguments, and devise effective plans for study. In addition to being essential for scientific invention and discovery, analytical thinking and the ability to solve problems are also quite significant.

Barriers to Critical Thinking

Emotional roadblocks: When it comes to critical thinking, one's emotions may be a huge obstacle. When people have a significant amount of emotional investment in a problem, it may be difficult for them to think objectively and assess facts in a rational manner. For instance, when a person is angry or disturbed, they may be more inclined to make hasty judgments or leap to conclusions without carefully analyzing all of the data. Individuals need to learn how to self-regulate their emotions and approach circumstances with a level head and an objective mentality in order to overcome the emotional obstacles that inhibit critical thinking.

Confirmation bias is the propensity to look for, analyze, and recall information in a manner that confirms pre-existing thoughts or attitudes. The term "confirmation bias" was coined by psychologists in the 1960s. Those who are subject to this bias may be less likely to examine alternate points of view or to evaluate facts in an impartial manner. Confirmation bias may be addressed if people make a conscious effort to seek out other points of view and give consideration to data that contradicts their existing beliefs.

People have views or assumptions about other people and the world around them that are influenced by their cultural upbringing or the experiences they have had in their culture. The way in which people process information and form judgments may be influenced by these biases, which often result in the establishment of stereotypes or prejudices. Individuals must be conscious of their own cultural background and make an active effort to learn about and comprehend the cultures and points of view of others in order to be successful in overcoming cultural prejudices.

Egocentrism is the inclination to perceive the world from one's own viewpoint and to feel that one's own opinions or experiences are more true or relevant than those of others. It is also the belief that one's own experiences are more important than those of others. Because of this, people may be less likely to explore alternative points of view or evaluate facts in an impartial manner. Individuals need to be ready to explore various points of view and open to new ideas and experiences in order to overcome their tendency toward egocentrism.

One of the most fundamental obstacles to critical thinking is ignorance, which may manifest itself as a deficiency in either knowledge or comprehension of a certain subject. It is possible for people to lack the ability to analyze evidence properly or make judgments based on that information if they do not have the essential underlying knowledge. People need to be eager to learn about the issue at hand and actively seek out information about it in order to break through this barrier.

Groupthink arises when a collection of persons gives more weight to reaching an agreement and maintaining harmony than they do to engaging in critical thinking or doing independent research. This may result in the silencing of alternative ideas and a dearth of inventive approaches to the resolution of issues. Individuals need to be ready to question the consensus of the group in order to foster independent thought and resist the effects of groupthink.

An unhealthy dependence on authoritative sources: An unhealthy reliance on authoritative sources, whether they be experts or other people, maybe a substantial impediment to critical thinking. People run the risk of missing crucial information or making erroneous conclusions when they give deference to authority figures or experts without challenging the assumptions they make or analyzing the facts. Individuals need to be ready to challenge those in power and assess data in a critical manner in order to get over this obstacle.

An unhealthy dependence on technology is becoming more common in this day and age because of the vital role that it now plays as a source of information and communication. Nonetheless, a dependency on technology to an unhealthy degree may be a roadblock to critical thinking. When people just depend on technology to obtain information or communicate, they run the risk of missing important information or failing to analyze evidence in an impartial manner. Individuals must be ready to seek out many sources of knowledge and interact directly with other people in order to overcome this obstacle.

CHAPTER 2

The Elements of Critical Thinking

Critical thinking is the process of analyzing data and supporting arguments in order to make reasoned conclusions or decisions. Getting a logical conclusion entails understanding and analyzing data, identifying biases and assumptions, and taking into account different viewpoints. To think critically and make wise decisions, a number of components that make up critical thinking must work together.

1. Knowledge: Critical thinking is built on knowledge. It entails having a thorough comprehension of the subject or problem at hand. People might not be able to examine facts efficiently or come to a logical conclusion if they lack the necessary information. Hence,

in order to be able to think critically, subject knowledge is necessary.

2. The analysis is the process of dissecting intricate information into its constituent elements in order to comprehend it better. Studying data enables people to spot patterns, correlations, and discrepancies that might not be immediately obvious. It entails examining data from a variety of aspects and viewpoints to create a more thorough grasp of the problem.

3. Drawing conclusions from the data at hand is the process of inference. It entails tying together disparate pieces of knowledge to arrive at a logical conclusion. Inference allows people to utilize their critical thinking abilities to assess the evidence and identify the most plausible explanation for the data.

4. Interpretation: Interpretation is the process of giving meaning to information in order to make sense of it. It entails taking into account the material's context and comprehending how the information may affect the current problem. While interpreting, people must exercise critical thinking to assess the data and make an informed opinion.

5. Evaluation is the process of determining if the information is reliable and pertinent. It entails evaluating the validity, reliability, and precision of the provided evidence. When evaluating, people must exercise critical thinking to examine, understand, and judge the information's applicability to the problem at hand.

6. Explanation: Explanation entails providing a succinct and unambiguous justification for a selected viewpoint or course of action. It requires applying critical thinking abilities to articulate an argument supported by reason and evidence. Those who want to explain something need to make their points succinctly and clearly, and they need to back up their arguments with facts.

7. Self-regulation entails keeping a close eye on one's own thoughts and decision-making processes. It entails being conscious of one's prejudices, presumptions, and limits and making an effort to get over them. Self-regulation calls on people to continuously assess their own thought and decision-making processes using critical thinking abilities.

CHAPTER 3

The Steps in Critical Thinking

Step 1: Identifying the Issue

The first thing that needs to be done in order to practice critical thinking is to pinpoint the issue or problem that needs to be solved. In order to accomplish this, it is necessary to first acknowledge the existence of a problem and then precisely define it. In order for people to identify the problem, they need to be very explicit and specific about the issue that they are attempting to fix.

Step 2: Collect the Necessary Information

The following phase, which comes after the problem has been identified, is to collect information that is connected to the problem. This requires individuals to collect data, facts, and evidence that can assist others in developing a better understanding of the issue. Individuals must maintain an open mind and be willing to examine information obtained from a range of sources in order to gather knowledge successfully.

Step 3: Evaluate the Information

The next phase, following the acquisition of information, is to analyze it in a critical manner. This requires conducting an analysis and providing an interpretation of the material in order to establish its trustworthiness, relevance, and accuracy. In order to judge the quality of the evidence that is provided, individuals need to be able to employ their critical thinking skills while evaluating information.

Step 4: Identify any assumptions.

In order to engage in critical thinking, it is necessary to first recognize and analyze one's assumptions. Beliefs or concepts that people accept without question but may not be aware that they do so are examples of assumptions. In order for individuals to identify their own beliefs and biases, as well as the assumptions that underlie their thinking, they must first evaluate their own beliefs and assumptions.

Step 5: Evaluate Arguments

The following phase, which comes after the identification of assumptions, is to assess the arguments that have been offered. This entails doing an investigation into the evidence offered as well as evaluating the soundness and dependability of the arguments. Individuals need to be able to apply critical thinking abilities in order to evaluate the quality of the evidence that is offered in order to evaluate arguments.

Step 6: Draw conclusions.

The process of arriving at a judgment or choice that is informed and based on the information and evidence that was offered is referred to as drawing conclusions. This requires compiling all of the relevant facts and evidence into a coherent whole in order to come up with a logical argument or answer. To be able to draw conclusions, individuals need to be able to apply their critical thinking skills to analyze the facts and come to a judgment that is logical and well-informed.

Step 7: Contemplate the Whole Procedure

In critical thinking, the final stage is to reflect on the process that was followed. This entails determining the strengths and weaknesses of the critical thinking process in order to locate areas that need to be improved. Individuals must first be self-aware and acknowledge their own biases and limits before they can effectively reflect on the process.

Chapter 4

Developing Critical Thinking Skills

The cultivation of skills in critical thinking is a crucial component of both personal and professional development. It is the process of deliberately and methodically assessing information, data, and ideas in order to arrive at decisions and judgments that are well-informed. The capacity for critical thinking is a skill that is valuable in many different professions, including business, education, healthcare, and government. In this piece, we will talk about how important it is to build critical thinking skills and provide some helpful advice on how to do so practically.

Why is it Necessary to Build Critical Thinking Skills?

The ability to think critically is absolutely necessary for success in the current world. They provide individuals with the ability to analyze difficult situations, make judgments based on relevant information, and effectively solve issues. The following are some of the many reasons why it is necessary to develop critical thinking skills:

Improved Capacity for Making Decisions

Those who are skilled in critical thinking are better able to make educated decisions that are founded on evidence and logical reasoning. They make it possible for individuals to examine many points of view and consider the benefits and drawbacks of various solutions. People are able to steer clear of quick and rash actions that can have unfavorable repercussions if they exercise their capacity for critical thinking.

Better Problem Solving

The ability to think critically is absolutely necessary for successful issue resolution. They give people the ability to break down difficult situations into manageable components, recognize underlying difficulties, and devise effective solutions. Individuals are able to approach problems in a systematic manner, take into consideration a variety of perspectives, and evaluate the success of their answers when they use critical thinking.

Improved Creative Capacity

Those who have developed their critical thinking skills are better equipped to think creatively and come up with original solutions to challenges. They inspire individuals to think creatively, evaluate issues from a variety of angles, and come up with original concepts. Individuals are able to investigate novel alternatives and come up with inventive solutions when they engage in critical thinking.

Enhanced Capabilities of Communicating

The ability to think critically is absolutely necessary for effective communication. They make it possible for people to articulate their thoughts in a way that is crystal clear and rational, listen intently to the perspectives of others, and carry on fruitful conversations. People are able to successfully interact with one another, clarify their own ideas, and steer clear of misunderstandings when they use critical thinking.

Heightened levels of self-awareness

Those who have developed the capacity of critical thinking are able to reflect on their own thought processes, identify their own biases and preconceptions, and cultivate a more nuanced view of themselves and others. Individuals are able to become more self-aware, recognize areas in which they may grow, and acquire a more open-minded and empathic perspective when they engage in critical thinking.

Advice on How to Improve Your Critical Thinking Abilities

Building one's capacity for critical thinking is a process that continues throughout one's life and calls for consistent practice and commitment. The following are some helpful hints that will assist you in developing your analytical thinking skills:

Ask Questions

In order to engage in critical thinking, it is essential to ask questions. It gives people the ability to make their thinking more clear, question their beliefs, and analyze the evidence. Asking questions with open-ended answers, considering a variety of viewpoints, and looking for evidence to support your findings are all great ways to build your critical thinking skills.

Examine Evidence

Assessing the reliability of one's sources is an essential component of critical thinking. It entails determining the accuracy and dependability of the material, locating any preconceived notions or prejudices, and weighing the facts in favor of a variety of diverse points of view. Assess evidence from a variety of sources, take into account the credibility and validity of the material, and apply logical reasoning to evaluate the persuasive power of the arguments. Doing so will help you build your critical thinking skills.

Think about things from a variety of angles.

For the development of skills in critical thinking, it is vital to take into consideration a variety of perspectives. It gives people the ability to investigate situations from a variety of perspectives, question their own presumptions, and acquire a more nuanced understanding of complicated topics as a result. To improve your ability to think critically, you should think about issues from a variety of angles, seek out people with varying points of view, and have respectful conversations with people who hold differing points of view.

Practice your ability to reason logically.

The cultivation of skills in logical reasoning is essential for the development of effective critical thinking. Finding patterns, conducting data analysis, and making inferences based on the findings are all part of the process. In order to improve your ability to think critically, you should exercise logical reasoning by working through puzzles, examining data sets, and determining the relationships between causes and effects.

Think about What You've Been Thinking

The ability to build critical thinking skills is inextricably linked to the practice of reflecting on one's own thoughts.

Evaluating your own presuppositions and biases, locating areas in which you may make improvements, and cultivating a more self-aware and nuanced perspective are all required steps.

Chapter 5

Applying Critical Thinking in Different Situations

Critical thinking is an important talent that helps individuals to study and evaluate information, facts, and ideas so that they may make decisions and judgments based on that analysis and evaluation. This is a talent that is important in many different professions, including business, education, healthcare, and government, among others. In this post, we will explain how the ability to think critically may be employed in a variety of different contexts.

Using Analytical Reasoning in Commercial Contexts

Critical thinking is a crucial skill for businesspeople to have in order to make educated decisions and find solutions to difficult challenges. It gives people the ability to examine data, consider many possibilities, and see chances for innovation and progress. In the corporate world, critical thinking may be useful in a variety of contexts, including the following:

Making a Plan for the Future

A skill set that includes critical thinking is very necessary for successful strategic planning. They provide people the ability to examine data, evaluate patterns, and find chances for development and expansion in their businesses. Business leaders are able to establish successful plans that are aligned with the aims and objectives of their organizations when they use critical thinking to do so.

Making a Call or a Choice

Having strong abilities in critical thinking is absolutely necessary for making sound decisions in the corporate world. They make it possible for humans to assess many possibilities, consider the benefits and drawbacks of a variety of solutions, and arrive at well-informed conclusions based on rational evidence and deductive reasoning. Business leaders may avoid making rash and ill-considered choices that could have unfavorable repercussions by using their capacity for critical thinking.

Problem-Solving

The ability to think critically is absolutely necessary for addressing problems successfully in business. They provide people with the ability to break down difficult situations into manageable components, recognize underlying difficulties, and devise effective solutions. When leaders in business make use of critical thinking, they are better able to approach challenges in a methodical manner, take into account a variety of views, and assess the efficiency of their solutions.

Innovation

The ability to think critically is absolutely necessary for promoting innovation in business. They provide individuals with the ability to think creatively, explore a variety of views, and come up with original concepts. Leaders in business are in a better position to differentiate their companies from those of their rivals when they apply critical thinking and explore new avenues of possibility and come up with unique solutions.

Implementing Reflective Thinking in Educational Settings

In the field of education, critical thinking is absolutely necessary for the growth of the intellectual and cognitive capacities of pupils. Students are able to solve issues, analyze and evaluate information, and make judgments based on that analysis and evaluation. The following are some applications of critical thinking that may be found in educational settings:

Curriculum Development

The ability to think critically is absolutely necessary for the creation of a successful curriculum. They make it possible for teachers to construct a curriculum that develops students' capacities for critical thinking, involves students in meaningful learning experiences, and is in line with the educational goals and objectives. The use of critical thinking by educators allows for the creation of curriculums that better prepare students for future success in their chosen fields of work.

The Art of Teaching and Learning

Having abilities in critical thinking is absolutely necessary for designing successful education. They provide teachers the ability to create learning experiences that keep students interested, encourage critical thinking, and cater to a variety of pupils' preferred methods of instruction. The use of critical thinking by educators enables the development of instructional techniques that improve students' academic performance and make it easier for students to acquire new material.

The Processes of Assessment and Evaluation

Skills in critical thinking are absolutely necessary for accurate assessment and evaluation in the field of education. They make it possible for educators to construct exams that measure students' critical thinking abilities, offer feedback that promotes students' learning and evaluate the efficacy of teaching practices through the use of these tools. The use of critical thinking by educators enables the creation of exams that more precisely evaluate the cognitive capacities of pupils and contribute to the student's academic performance.

Using Analytical Reasoning in the Healthcare System

In the field of healthcare, the ability to think critically is necessary in order to provide high-quality treatment for patients. It gives medical personnel the ability to examine data, identify diseases, and devise treatment regimens that are both effective and efficient. The following are a few illustrations of how critical thinking may be utilized in the medical field:

Diagnosis

Skills in critical thinking are absolutely necessary for accurate diagnosis in the healthcare field. They make it possible for medical experts to examine the symptoms of patients, analyze the data, and determine the illnesses that are behind those symptoms. Critical thinking enables medical practitioners to arrive at correct diagnoses, which in turn leads to the development of successful therapies.

The Planning of Therapy

Skills in critical thinking are absolutely necessary for efficient treatment planning in the healthcare industry. They make it possible for medical practitioners to establish treatment plans that cater to the specific requirements of patients, take into account the potential drawbacks and advantages of a variety of interventions, and are in line with the patients' objectives and preferences. Critical thinking enables medical practitioners to establish treatment regimens that maximize the health and well-being of their patients.

CHAPTER 6

Avoiding Common Pitfalls in Critical Thinking

In this section, we will discuss some of the most typical problems associated with critical thinking and offer techniques for avoiding those errors.

Confirmation Bias

Confirmation bias is a common pitfall in critical thinking that occurs when individuals seek out information that confirms their pre-existing beliefs and ignores information that contradicts their beliefs. This occurs when individuals seek out information that confirms their pre-existing beliefs and ignores information that contradicts their beliefs. This bias can lead to thinking that is too restricted, having limited viewpoints, and making decisions that are not optimal. The following actions should be taken by individuals to avoid confirmation bias:

1. Be conscious of their pre-existing viewpoints, ideas, and prejudices.
2. Investigate a wide range of resources for various types of data.
3. Analyze the facts in a way that is objective without taking into account any personal opinions or biases.
4. Think about things from different vantage points and points of view.

Groupthink is discussed

The critical thinking trap, known as groupthink, happens when individuals adapt to the beliefs and ideas of a group, regardless of whether or not those thoughts and ideas are erroneous. Groupthink is a typical mistake in critical thinking. This trap can lead to uniformity, which in turn can lead to limited creative expression and poor decision-making. Individuals, in order to prevent falling prey to groupthink, should:

1. Promote a variety of thoughts, perspectives, and ideas.
2. Put the established order and conventional modes of thought to the test.
3. Promote dialogue that is both open and truthful.
4. Analyze the facts in an objective manner, without taking into consideration the pressure or the consensus of the group.

Oversimplification of the Situation

Overgeneralization is a frequent fallacy in critical thinking that arises when individuals draw broad generalizations based on inadequate facts or experience. This may be dangerous since it can lead to incorrect conclusions. This trap may easily lead to erroneous assumptions, bias, and poor decision-making. To prevent making too broad of statements, people should:

1. Be conscious of the minimal evidence or experience they have to provide.
2. Investigate the possibility of uncovering further details and proof.
3. Think about the possibility of other explanations and points of view.

4. Be clear about drawing sweeping generalizations based on a small number of facts or experiences.

Emotional Reasoning

When people make decisions or conclusions based on their emotions rather than reason and facts, they engage in emotional reasoning, which is a prevalent fallacy in critical thinking. Emotional reasoning can happen for a number of reasons. This trap can lead to skewed thinking, poor decision-making, and illogical action on the part of the individual. To stay away from making decisions based on their emotions, individuals should:

1. Be conscious of their feelings and the ways in which those feelings may be affecting the way they think.

2. Analyze the data dispassionately, paying no attention to your own feelings or preconceptions.
3. Think about the possibility of other explanations and points of view.
4. Instead of depending simply on feelings, make decisions and judgments by making use of reason and evidence instead.

A Generalization Made in Haste

When people draw broad generalizations based on scant or insufficient data, they are committing the critical thinking fallacy known as hasty generalization. This is a typical trap that many people fall into. This trap can easily lead to poor decision-making, which in turn can lead to incorrect conclusions. Individuals should avoid making hasty generalizations by doing the following:

1. Be mindful that their proof is either inadequate or insufficient.
2. Investigate the possibility of uncovering further details and proof.
3. Think about the possibility of other explanations and points of view.
4. To avoid drawing sweeping generalizations based on scant or insufficient data, please refrain from doing so.

Ad Hominem Attacks

Ad hominem attacks are a typical fallacy in critical thinking that arise when individuals attack the person presenting an argument rather than the argument itself. Ad hominem attacks may be avoided by avoiding the common trap of attacking the person making the argument. This trap may easily lead to skewed thinking, poor decision-making, and even assaults on the individual. Individuals should avoid using ad hominem arguments by doing the following:

1. Pay attention to the point being said rather than the individual who is delivering the point.
2. Analyze the evidence dispassionately, ignoring any personal preferences or convictions you may have.
3. Think about the possibility of other explanations and points of view.
4. Instead of depending exclusively on insults directed at the speaker, assess the arguments using logic and supporting facts.

The Fallacy of Choosing Between Two Options

A false dichotomy is a common fallacy in critical thinking that arises when individuals provide just two options as if they are the only conceivable choices. This occurs when individuals present only two options as if they are the only potential choices.

Chapter 7

Enhancing Critical Thinking Through Practice

Participate in attentive listening behavior.

Critical thinking relies heavily on attentive listening, which is a skill in and of itself. When a person listens attentively, they are more likely to be able to recognize assumptions, analyze data, and take into consideration various points of view. Those who want to improve their critical thinking through active listening should do the following:

1. Pay attention to what the speaker is saying and stay away from distractions.

2. In order to have a better comprehension, ask questions.
3. Conduct a dispassionate analysis of the claims made by the speaker and the supporting evidence.
4. Think about things from different vantage points and points of view.

Ask Questions

In order to engage in critical thinking, it is necessary to ask questions. Individuals may detect assumptions, analyze data, and examine alternate views simply by engaging in questioning behavior. Those who want to improve their critical thinking via questioning should do the following:

1. Use open-ended questions to foster conversation

2. In order to unearth the underlying prejudices and preconceptions, ask penetrating questions.
3. In order to guarantee that there is comprehension, you should ask clarifying questions.
4. Ask questions to examine the evidence objectively

Analyze Evidence

Assessing the reliability of one's sources is an essential part of critical thinking. If a person makes an objective assessment of the data presented to them, they are more likely to make decisions and judgments that are informed. Those who want to improve their critical thinking by analyzing evidence should do the following:

1. Determine the trustworthiness of the evidence's sources after you've identified them.
2. Assess the quality of the evidence as well as its relevance.
3. Think about the possibility of other explanations and points of view.
4. While assessing the validity of evidence, you should not factor in your own preferences or views.

Consider a Number of Different Points of View

While engaging in critical thinking, it is essential to take into account a variety of different points of view. Individuals are able to get a more comprehensive grasp of a subject and objectively assess arguments when they take into consideration other points of view. Those who want to improve their critical thinking by studying a variety of viewpoints should do the following:

1. Explore a wide range of resources to obtain viewpoints that differ from your own.
2. Think about this in a variety of different historical, cultural, and social situations.
3. Analyze the contentions in a manner that is objective, without regard to your own preferences or convictions.
4. Determine the areas in which we are in agreement and disagreement.

Evaluate the Presuppositions

The process of critically examining one's assumptions is an essential part of the critical thinking process. When people are able to recognize their preconceptions, they are in a better position to analyze data in an impartial manner and explore various points of view. Those who want to improve their critical thinking by evaluating assumptions should do the following:

1. Find the assumptions and judge whether or not they are correct.
2. Think about situations and viewpoints that differ from your own.
3. Analyze the evidence dispassionately, ignoring any personal preferences or convictions you may have.
4. Avoid forming judgments about things based on insufficient evidence or experience.

Practice and Reflection

The ability to think critically may be significantly improved via the practice of reflection. Those who take the time to reflect on their own thought processes are better able to recognize weak spots in their reasoning and provide ideas for how they might enhance their capacity for critical thought. Those who want to improve their critical thinking via contemplation should do the following:

1. Consider their mental processes and the ways in which they make decisions.
2. Determine which aspects need to be improved.
3. Create methods that will help you improve your critical thinking abilities.

4. Assess the efficiency of various tactics throughout the course of time.

Participate in Problem-Solving Strategies

The use of critical thinking in a more practical setting is problem-solving. Problem-solving provides individuals with the opportunity to apply their critical thinking abilities to circumstances that occur in the real world. Individuals should do the following in order to improve their critical thinking through the process of issue-solving:

1. Determine the difficulties that exist and the extent of those problems.
2. Collect information and be critical of the evidence you find.

3. Produce a variety of potential other solutions, then assess how successful they are.
4. Apply and assess the effectiveness of the remedies throughout time.

CONCLUSION

Anybody who is interested in developing and improving their critical thinking abilities will find "Mastering Critical Thinking: The Art of Logical Problem Solving" to be an invaluable resource. This book offers a thorough introduction to critical thinking, including not only the components of critical thinking as well as its phases but also the major errors that readers should try to avoid. The reader will also benefit from the inclusion of practical tasks and examples that help them use their critical thinking abilities in a variety of contexts.

To improve one's capacity for critical thinking, the author places a strong emphasis throughout the text on the following methods: active listening; questioning; evaluating evidence;

considering alternative points of view; analyzing assumptions; practicing reflection; and engaging in problem-solving activities. Readers may become better decision-makers, problem-solvers, and critical thinkers if they master the abilities listed below.

Those who are interested in improving their critical thinking abilities will find "Mastering Critical Thinking: The Art of Logical Problem Solving" to be a good resource overall. This book offers a good road map for developing the abilities essential to think critically and successfully solving challenges, making it useful for both personal and professional growth.

www.ingramcontent.com/pod-product-compliance
Lightning Source LLC
Chambersburg PA
CBHW071140220526
45467CB00015B/1651